Dear Kristin,

I hope this book brings you moments of peace on the difficult days and joy on the days you feel good!

With love,

♡ + Horia

Rest & Return

WEEKLY REMINDERS TO PAUSE, REFLECT, AND JUST BE

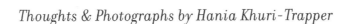

Thoughts & Photographs by Hania Khuri-Trapper

ISBN: 978-1-09-839876-7

FOR MORE INFORMATION:
www.YogawithHania.com

Foreword

I have a collection of Hania's notes in various piles. These notes include affirmations, quotes, and yoga sutras she chose as a thread for a particular week of yoga instruction. As offerings, Hania's affirmations served as tangible reminders that life is to be lived fully, no matter the struggles or celebrations. Some of the notes I collected can be found stained with tea in the cup holder in my car. Others serve as placeholders in various books I'm reading that teeter on my night table. I even found a stash of these notes in my kit of essential oils and they are now soaked with a touch of citrus, frankincense or lavender. I have gathered Hania's notes after years of attending her yoga classes—sometimes grabbing an extra swatch for a daughter or friend in need. I even included one of Hania's personal stories she shared in a class in my book, *The Kindness Cure*, as a simple lesson in ordinary kindness.

It's the personal that is so present in this extraordinary collection of photographs and vignettes. It's one thing to share the wise words of others, which Hania selected with such care; it's another to pour your heart onto the pages like a poet. *Rest and Return* is simply a delight to the senses. Each page exudes a tenderness and vulnerability that is both revealing and reassuring. My first read was one of sensorial delight; my second read was a recognition of the common humanity that ties us together in the here and now. My third read, an enchanting exercise at landing on a random selection, revealed the deeply human need for self-love and acceptance. I have no doubt that you, the lucky reader, will be touched by the following pages in one way or another and be drawn into the magical power of being present.

Rest and Return is both timeless and timely. Every era is marked by uncertainty and tragedy as it is also marked by resilience and compassion. *Rest and Return* is a reminder to all of us that the present moment is all we have and offers us a choice on how to respond to whatever unfolds. Hania writes, "When we are aligned with the present, we are grateful, we are at peace, we find acceptance with ourselves exactly how we are." May you find what is clear and true in your life as you leaf through these pages in wonder.

— Tara Cousineau, PhD

Author of *The Kindness Cure: How the Science of Compassion Can Heal Your Heart and Your World*

Introduction

Why this book? Why now?

I have never fancied myself a writer or a photographer or even a teacher, but somehow this is where my path has led. The inspiration for this book comes from a simple quote by the spiritual teacher Ram Dass: "We are all just walking each other home." To me, this quote represents the shared experience of moving together through life, bringing what we know to those around us and sharing our greatest gifts.

When my father was sick with a brain tumor, I felt the need to dive deeper into my yoga practice. When he passed, I grieved on my mat over and over again until I came to peace with his passing. Yoga helped. It was the gift of space, the gift of permission to show up and not be okay. The mat became my shelter, my safety net, my ground. The movement helped shift stuck, raw, and tired energy through my body. My breath kept me steady and reminded me to slow down enough to appreciate each one and be present. All of these tools together helped me heal. They reminded me that the suffering is part of our lives but so is the healing. And it was during that healing process that I decided to become a yoga teacher so I could share what helped me with others.

For the last 11 years or so I have crafted weekly classes inspired by different teachers and thinkers I have studied along the way. Each class is anchored with a quote that shares the message of the week. Throughout my teaching, I expand upon these messages with my own perspective, adding the physical movements of yoga to complement the theme.

Then the COVID-19 pandemic rocked the world, bringing life as we know it to a screeching halt. Life for me slowed down to an unrecognizable pace. And the themes of slowing down, adapting and building a reservoir of resilience eclipsed everything in my path until that point.

The woods became an extension of my yoga practice. During the height of the lockdown, every day I entered the woods, took a deep breath and saw something new. Every day I learned a little bit more about myself. The woods knew my struggles and my joys and received me without judgment, opening my eyes each time to a new palette or texture that I'd never seen before.

And just when the colors started to blend and look the same, that's when I heard the woodpecker or the creaking tree that wanted to fall over and rest on the ground after the storm took away its will. So many turns, so many choices of which way to go.

Inspired by the adaptability and resilience of the woods, I created an online platform to continue to teach yoga to my students. Each Friday, I would send them a recording of my yoga class and the weekly message. After over a year and a half, I realized that I had all of this content that I wanted to share, along with all of the photographs that I had taken along the way. And because I'm a graphic designer by profession, I thought why not combine it all and share it with the world? If anything, I could finally house my deepest thoughts and imagery in one place. And if it helps just one person, then it was worth all of the effort and love that I have poured into these pages.

I hope you find a little nugget here to take with you to inspire your own life. And I hope you will reach out and share your thoughts with me. Because after all, "We are all just walking each other home."

SPECIAL THANKS...

So many people to thank for this project, but it all starts with my family. Chris, Sami, and Faris— my A-team who have always supported my slightly obsessive yogic and artistic whims; my mother Randa (my greatest teacher and cheerleader); my sister Maya and my brother Naseem (the choir singers); Malek, Sena, Zaid, Zia, Rami (the orchestra); the Virtual Kitchen Group; and all of my dear friends near and far who I consider family. Thank you. I have felt all of your generous spirits developing the words and photos of this book.

Thank you to Tara Cousineau for such kind words introducing "Rest & Return." Your book "The Kindness Cure" has a permanent place on my bedside table and in my teacher trainings. And thank you to Sarada Peri for having the incredibly challenging task of interpreting and editing my words. I am humbled and so very grateful for both of your contributions to this dream of mine.

"Hope is being able
to see that there
is light despite all
of the darkness."

—*Desmond Tutu*

Hope Starts Here...

Sometimes we have to experience the darkness
in our lives to move into the light.
But sometimes our own weight starts to bury us.
And it becomes easier to live in that darkness.
If we stay, we paralyze ourselves and don't grow.
We might think that baby birds wait until
they are fully ready and strong enough to fly
from the nest, but that's not always true.
Sometimes the nest becomes more dangerous,
more vulnerable to predators.
Their home as they know it is not a safe place to grow.

And their only choice is hope.

Hope that their wings will carry them.
Hope for a better life.
It's that hope that allows them to move
from darkness into light.
To find that well of courage
even when there is uncertainty and risk.
To choose that space of resilience instead of fear.

Let your hope be stronger than your fear.
Let your hope be so strong that it lifts you and
opens you up to the spaciousness in your being.
So that no matter where you are, you are free.

why not try .... *Notice if you feel the heaviness in your chest. Take a deep breath. Imagine that you're breathing in lightness. Let that lightness expand from your belly through your rib cage and up into your collarbones. Exhale. Release any tension you carry in your heart.*

Anchor in Your Breath

It is said that 90% of illness is due to stress. How do you avoid the stress that presents itself during such changing times with uncertainty all around? Think of your breath as an anchor that keeps you grounded in the midst of chaos. Even when waves move overhead, you are not deterred because you are grounded in the steady rhythm of the present moment. The world may feel like it's spinning out of control, but you don't have to. Anchor into your breath. Slow your pace so that you can remain clear. It's that clarity that builds resilience and allows you to manage those difficult and stressful times with grace. Carve out that time for YOU to build that steadiness and return home to the calm within you.

A great way to anchor your breath is through the **alternate nostril breathing technique** *(nadi shodhana pranayama, which loosely translates to gentle energy clearing breath). This technique clears and balances the energy channels, reduces stress, and balances the two sides of the body. Here's how to perform nadi shodhana:*

1. *With your right hand, place your thumb gently on your right nostril. Tuck your second and third finger down or place on your forehead.*
2. *Close your right nostril with your thumb and exhale fully through your left nostril. Keeping your thumb pressed on your right nostril, inhale fully through the left nostril.*
3. *Close the left nostril with your ring finger and exhale through the right nostril. Keeping your thumb pressed on your left nostril, inhale fully through the right nostril.*
4. *Repeat nine more rounds of even and steady alternate nostril breathing.*

......why not try

PRANAYAMA

STEP 1   STEP 2   STEP 3

"There is more to
life than increasing
its speed."
—*Mahatma Gandhi*

"The flower doesn't dream
of the bee. It blossoms
and the bee comes."

— *Mark Nepo*

Bloom and Receive

Have you ever had a relationship that made you give up your power? Or maybe you wanted a relationship to work so badly that you lost yourself along the way? I certainly have. I remember wanting so desperately to be loved that it felt painful when the feeling wasn't reciprocated. And the more I looked for that deep love outside of myself, the more fragmented, the more insignificant I felt. It wasn't until I gave myself space to heal and nurture that I felt whole again.

That is how I learned that happiness cannot be found by holding onto people, places or things. Happiness is an inside job. When you begin the work of nurturing yourself, listening and following your inner voice, you can bloom and be heard.

It's not easy to show up for yourself and do the work, but when you connect to YOU—your body, your mind, your breath—you can blossom and receive all the good that you deserve... and that is precisely the moment when the bee arrives.

why not try

PRANAYAMA

*Pranayama is awareness and control of breath. It is one of the eight limbs of yoga. There is a Pranayama exercise called **"Bee Breath"** (Bhramari Pranayama). Here's the simplest method...*

- *Find a comfortable seat, relax your body and close your eyes.*
- *Close your lips softly so that you can still feel air coming out of your mouth.*
- *Bring your right index finger to your right ear flap and your left index finger to your left ear flap and gently close both flaps so you cannot hear.*
- *Take a deep inhale into the nose and exhale making a buzzing sound until there is no air left.*
- *Take 5 rounds of this humming bee breath to connect to your deeper self.*

Stand Your Ground

What does it mean to feel grounded? In life, sometimes it feels like someone pulled the rug from underneath you. And it seems as though everything is spinning out of control. That feeling can be compared to watching the little particles in a shaken snow globe that cloud and obscure the image at the center. When your center seems to be lost and you feel scattered, it is difficult to focus and to perform everyday duties, let alone to feel calm and grounded.

The purpose of yoga according to Yoga Sutra 1.2 is *yogas chitta vritti nirodha*, which translates to 'yoga is the mastery or control of the thought patterns of the mind.' The word *vritti* literally means to whirl around just like the little particles in the snow globe. The yoga sutras examine how to calm the mind and find clarity through a holistic approach to life. One of many such tools is the physical yoga practice. Whenever I feel that scattered energy and lack of focus, I take a moment to find stillness and stand firmly on the ground. Whenever I root down, and take a few moments to calm, I'm able to gather my strength so I can rise and meet the moment.

....why not try

YOGA POSE

__Mountain Pose__ (tadasana) is the foundational yoga pose for all of the standing postures. Here's how to stand your ground and grow tall:

- *Stand tall with your feet together (toes touching, heels can be slightly apart).*
- *Ground down through all four corners of your feet.*
- *Draw your shoulder blades down your back and lengthen through your spine.*
- *Extend your arms by your side and let your palms face forward. Your whole body is active and your gaze is steady.*
- *Just for a moment, stand how you normally stand (usually leaning on one hip and with your shoulders folding forward). Now come back to mountain pose. Notice how much more powerful you feel!*

"Be sure you put your feet in the right place, then stand firm."

— *Abraham Lincoln*

"You are on the path... exactly where you are meant to be right now... And from here, you can only go forward, shaping your life story into a magnificent tale of triumph, of healing of courage, of beauty, of wisdom, of power, of dignity, and of love." — *Caroline Adams*

The Labyrinth

Slow it down.
There's no rush.
Sometimes life brings everything
to a screeching halt.
A forced pause, to make us look down
at our feet, and feel the ground.
To notice the sound of the chipping sparrow,
or the echo of the great horned owl.
If you listen long enough, you may
hear the rest of the symphony.

One mindful step at a time.
No need to say a word.
Follow the path.
Embrace the beauty in each moment,
and enjoy the silence within.

Occasionally the path gets too narrow
and it is difficult to balance.
Maybe you even fall over?
But the path reminds you
to get back up and keep moving.
Occasionally openings appear
making it easier to move quickly,
to rush along.

But then the path narrows,
a reminder to focus,
with steadiness and ease.

The end of the path seems so far away,
and the work seems endless.
But you return your eyes down to your feet,
to your steady breath.

One mindful step at a time.
No need to say a word.
Follow the path.
Embrace the beauty in each moment,
and enjoy the silence within.

But it's when you take your last step,
arriving at the center of the labyrinth,
that you realize the journey itself was the goal.
That beauty was present in the moments
of losing balance, of struggle,
and in the peaceful moments of ease.

Bringing all of that awareness with you
into the world, you leave the center
and make the journey home to where you began.

learn more......*The Labyrinth is the ancient tradition of a walking meditation to calm the mind and find clarity. Labyrinths exist in communities all across the world—there might even be one near you. Here's how they work: First, set an intention and walk around the perimeter in a clockwise direction. As you go, spin the Tibetan prayer wheels with your right hand to the left. When you have completed the circle, you are ready to enter and walk mindfully, following the path until you come to the center. Take as much sacred time as you need at the center. Then, follow the path out from the center back the way you came and when you reach the entrance repeat the walk around the perimeter in the same clockwise direction to give thanks for the experience and gratitude for the space. The beauty of the Labyrinth is that you can bring this same intentionality to any walk or hike, using it as a moving meditation.*

Strength and Connection from Balance

The yoga practice is a union of opposites:
ground down to reach high;
with effort, bring in ease;
move your body and then find stillness;
tune into your will and then let go;
inhale and exhale.

In April 2020, during the COVID-19 pandemic, hikers in the woods near my house began rock stacking as a way to leave their mark and create a little art. Others began to participate, adding to the existing "sculptures." The physical act of stacking rocks required true presence and sensitivity to balance. It was a simple way of finding order in a chaotic world. And it became a method of connection in a lonely and difficult time. From a place of isolation, people's need for community inspired creativity and humanity. So even in the woods by yourself, you were supported by your fellow hikers, and part of a greater community.

People seek balance wherever they are… physical, emotional, and spiritual. And sometimes the only way to know balance is to experience imbalance. Start by noticing the imbalances and the struggles you feel in this moment. Once you can identify the areas that feel off-balance, that's when the work begins. Because balance isn't something you just find along the way. It is like finding the perfect rock at an imperfect time and lifting it regardless of the weight and placing it upon the rock before it, with purpose and steadiness. Once you take a step back to view what you have created, you realize you moved though another challenge. And maybe then, take rest.

"Balance is not something you find, it's something you create."

—*Jana Kingsford*

"The most basic and powerful way to connect to another person is to listen. Just listen. Perhaps the most important thing we ever give each other is our attention."

— *Rachel Naomi Remen*

Why Listen?

When you listen, you are still.
When you listen, you separate from your ego.
When you listen, you learn a thing or two.

You strengthen the muscle of empathy,
And lengthen the muscle of patience.

You allow others to feel seen and heard.
And when others are seen and heard, they soften.
And when they soften, they relinquish their armor.
When the armor is gone, you see each other's humanity.

And when your humanity is exposed, your heart expands
And you see yourself in the other's eyes.

Taking time for stillness allows you to separate yourself from all of the noise, news, emotions, situations—and just be still. Still enough to hear beyond the noise and the loud pressures that you feel all around you. Still enough to slow down enough to hear your body speaking through the tightness and rigidity. And when you listen deeply, you learn how to respond with softness and ease. And underneath the tension, you tap into the raw emotions which, when held onto, cause suffering and stress in the deepest parts of your body. Listening brings clarity and understanding. Listening leads to a deeper connection of self.

why not try ...... *Find a comfortable seat and close your eyes. Find an alert spine and soften your shoulders. With your eyes closed, take a few moments for stillness. Get quiet enough to explore the sensations and listen to what the body is telling you. Then bring attention to your breath and listen to the natural flow of your breath. Keep this quiet focus on the sound and rhythm of your breath for as long as you think you need.*

Antidote to Stress

We all know the frustration of waiting in line when you are in a hurry. Or trying to remain calm when your child is being willful and unreasonable. These moments are everyday occurrences that build up stress in the body and mind. Stress is when you are somewhere, but long to be somewhere else. It's that longing that keeps you from your true nature. From your peace.

Patience is the antidote to stress. But the work is difficult. And often you are not even aware of it until you realize that you are being impatient. But patience is not about waiting idly. It is an active process of cultivating awareness of your thoughts and regulating your body with your breath. Both can be controlled and effectively mastered. So, the next time you notice yourself with a tight fuse, stop for a moment. Bring awareness to what's happening. Ask yourself if anything can be done to change the situation. And if not, soften into the moment. Keep your breath slow and steady.

...... why not try

When you are standing in line at the store and the person in front of you seems to be taking much longer than you feel is the appropriate length of time, remind yourself that not everyone is on your same schedule. And that maybe the person in front of you is your teacher of patience for the day. So instead of letting the stress build in your body, release your shoulders and take a slow breath in and an even longer slow breath out. Notice what happens to you emotionally when your body softens. By now that person in front of you is probably done with their transaction.

"Patience is not simply the ability to wait — it's how we behave while we're waiting."

—*Joyce Meyer*

"The art of life is a
constant readjustment
to our surroundings."
— *Kakuzo Okakaura*

Wisdom of a Tree

It has been said the measure of intelligence is the ability to change.

You can learn a great deal from the intelligence and wisdom of a tree. When the bark of the tree becomes wounded or infected, the tree keeps growing around the infection, sealing the area and creating a boundary of protection so the new growth is not at risk. The tree keeps moving onward and upward while navigating the difficulties in its path with a steadiness that only nature understands.

It is when you are confronted with uncertainty that you truly discover who you are. In that space is where growth and innovation thrive and where you learn that you are stronger and more resilient than you ever knew before.

why not try...... Here is a simple 3-step method to move through challenging times:

Triple A's to Navigate Uncertainty:

AWARE — Create awareness around your situation by stepping outside yourself and observing with a broader, 360-degree view. Can you notice what is true in the present moment without placing judgments or attachments to the experience?

ADAPT — Once you are aware of your situation, try not to get stuck or paralyzed. Instead, use that awareness to understand your situation and work with it. Allow yourself to adjust and move.

ACCEPT — Realize that everything is impermanent. Uncertainty is part of life and when we accept that fundamental truth, we suffer less. Acceptance reminds us that everything will change again and again.

Fall Forward

What's holding you back? The fear of failing? The fear of falling? Sometimes it feels like life is holding you back. And it's hard to understand why things seem beyond your control. But it is in those reflective moments that you can map your route and find clarity for where you want to go, even if you can't see the destination. When you bring awareness to your life, you don't collapse into the past—you fall forward. Former President Obama said, "We need to go forward, but progress isn't always a straight line or a smooth path." Sometimes your arrow zig zags from side to side. Sometimes you miss your target altogether.

But here's a thought...
"Thomas Edison conducted 1,000 failed experiments. Did you know that?
I didn't either—because number 1,001 was the light bulb. Fall forward.
Every failed experiment is one step closer to success." —Denzel Washington

During the COVID 19 pandemic, everyone wanted to go back to "normal." Normal was a place people knew, a familiar space. But the only way you can go back is to "fall forward." Falling forward is like that moment when you draw a bow pulling an arrow backwards—this motion makes it look as though the arrow is taking a step back instead of moving forward. But actually, with the arrow pulled back, you can see your target more clearly—and you gain the strength and momentum to move forward. Then, at the right moment, you can let go and the arrow moves forward. In the same way, falling back allows you to see more clearly. You are only there for a moment or two, but in that stillness, your gaze is forward and you can clearly see what's ahead. That's the moment you decide what you want to bring with you into the future, and what you want to let go of from our past. Either way, you move forward toward your goal with skill and intention.

> *Be clear. Do the work. Take risks. Try. Fail and try again.* ......*note to self*
> *The hardest step is always the first one.*

"Fall forward. Every failed experiment is one step closer to success."

— *Denzel Washington*

"If you are depressed
you are living in the past.
If you are anxious
you are living in the future.
If you are at peace you are
living in the present."

— *Lao Tzu*

Access the Present

A reporter once asked His Holiness the Dalai Lama what his happiest moment was. He simply said, "Right now."

The most effective way to combat stress and anxiety is to return home to this moment; to tune in to what you can control. Being present develops your spiritual muscles. When we are aligned with the present, we are grateful, we are at peace, we find acceptance with ourselves exactly how we are.

Happiness exists in real time.

So how do we access the present? Awareness is the key to combatting the anxiety that comes from fearing the future, and the depression that comes from holding on to the past. Mind and body awareness lead to feeling safe and strong in this very moment.

note to self……

Because remember…
This moment is all we really have.
And in this moment you are the youngest you will be,
for the rest of your life.

See the Beauty

For the longest time, each night before I slept, I would look up at the chandelier over my bed. And every night it brought me joy. Such a simple thing, representing history, lightness, and elegance all combined into one to radiate and transform the room.

But one night I looked up and noticed that one strand of crystal beads was missing from the bottom tier. After that night, every time I gazed up at my beautiful chandelier, I didn't see the many dazzling beads that remained. All I saw was that one missing strand. All I saw was a flaw. All I saw was what was missing. How would I replace them? When would I get to it? I could feel myself getting irritated.

Many nights passed, and one day I looked up and instead of immediately being upset by such a small thing, I realized something. Why choose to see the one tiny flaw in an otherwise perfect picture? That was all it took. A simple moment of awareness to shift away from negativity and back to joy.

Sometimes it's the small things in life that teach you the greatest lessons. ...... *note to self*

"If you look at what you have in life, you'll always have more. If you look at what you don't have in life, you'll never have enough."

— *Oprah Winfrey*

"To be broken
is no reason to see
all things as broken."
— *Mark Nepo*

Trust Deeply

Ever have that day when, from the moment you wake up, everything seems to go wrong? All seems bleak? I had one of those the other day. My thoughts weighed heavily on me. Even things that I knew were fine and good seemed dark.

When we are in the middle of heavy feelings, heavy thoughts, the world seems dark around us. But there is still lightness in the world, in ourselves, even though it may not be visible in the moment. We just need to hold ourselves up and hold on for the short ride, knowing that the sun is always shining even though all we see are clouds. That there is an unlimited supply of love even when we are feeling isolated and alone. That we can trust the universe even when we feel betrayed.

YOGA POSE

why not try......

*Here's a yoga pose that is both grounding and uplifting. In **downward dog**, you hold yourself up, forming the shape of a mountain. This is a foundational yoga pose that builds strength and length in the body. Trust begins here...*

- *Start on all fours in tabletop pose with wrists under shoulders and knees under your hips.*
- *Walk your hands one handprint forward, spread your fingers wide and press down.*
- *Curl your back toes under, engage your core and lift your hips to the sky.*
- *Send your tailbone up and back to lengthen the spine (you may have to soften your knees to find that length).*
- *Release tension in your head, neck and shoulders and send your gaze back between your legs.*
- *Take a few rounds of steady breath and drop your knees to the mat gently when you wish to come out of the pose.*

Duet

There is a duet that occurs between fear and love.
Between how you want to embrace yourself
and the voice that says you're not good enough.
Oh fear, like the undertow,
you pull me back, drag me below the surface,
and hope that I stay still.

And I might be quiet for a moment or two.
I might be frozen to act and move,
but in stillness comes clarity.
Clarity is a return to the heart.

And just like that I am reminded
that love has more power.
Love heals and strengthens wherever it lives.
Love is the ocean.
Love is the music within.

And just like a miracle there is a shift
from fear to love as the duet plays its last note.
What's left is one voice...one love.

"We can either repeat
old fear based patterns,
or our suffering can awaken
us to a deeper wisdom
and greater love."

—*Tara Brach*

"There is something wonderfully bold and liberating about saying yes to our entire imperfect and messy life."

— *Tara Brach*

Perfectly Messy

You may have heard the saying, "Perfection is the enemy of progress." From my own experience as a perfectionist in certain aspects of my life, when I don't think I can do something well (or perfectly), I don't even try. Perfectionism creates unrealistic expectations that we can never meet. But then I remember this yoga practice which asks us to meet ourselves where we are in our flawed and imperfect state. Age helps with cultivating that acceptance for yourself. In my 20's, I didn't dare have friends over for dinner unless my house was immaculate and the menu was planned and prepared perfectly. After having children and experiencing more of life, I enjoy having people over at a moment's notice. And in those moments of seeing friends and sharing a meal, I have learned how to appreciate their company and not obsess about the appearance of things.

When we hold ourselves in the present moment without judgment, we have the ability to soften those ambitious expectations and find acceptance with what is. There is so much freedom in finding the contentment in the now. Is there somewhere in your life that you are holding back for fear of not succeeding? How hard would it be to let go of your inner critic and jump right in? You might just love what you discover.

YOGA POSE

why not try......

Any balance pose requires you to be present. **Tree pose** *(Vrksasana) brings you back to your center and builds strength along the way...*

- *Stand tall with your feet together.*
- *Bring your hands together at your heart.*
- *Press down into all four corners of your right foot.*
- *Turn your left knee out to the side and press your heel against your shin.*
- *Stay or slide the soul of your left foot to the shin or inner thigh (be mindful not to press your foot against the knee joint).*
- *Steady your gaze, engage your core, & focus on your breath— the three power tools of balance!*
- *Hands can stay at heart center or arms can reach to the sky.*
- *Switch sides.*

Carry & Cradle

How are you meeting the moment? Kelly G. Wilson, a professor of psychology at the University of Mississippi, gave a perfect metaphor for our suffering. If you gently hold and cradle a small cactus in your hand, you can feel the spikes and notice the texture without discomfort. But if you were to take that same cactus and grab a hold of it tightly and squeeze it, you will feel incredible pain. It is the same with the suffering that we hold and keep within ourselves. We know that suffering is part of life, but are we responding and holding on tightly to more pain than is necessary? Maybe our suffering is not what we are carrying but how we are carrying it. When we learn to soften, we respond to our pain from a place of ease. We acknowledge the pain we hold, but we soften the grip, cradle our struggles and try not to attach to them. We forgive—ourselves, others—and find the path towards peace.

The "king" pose of the yoga practice is Savasana.
The Sanskrit word translates to Sava (corpse) and Asana (pose). The stillness allows the body rhythms and temperature to drop back to normal, enabling the parasympathetic nervous system to calm the body further. It gives you permission to let go of your thoughts and to rest in compassionate awareness. There's no more control; your breath returns back its natural state.

Lie on your back, close your eyes and feel the weight of your body. Take a few moments to scan your entire body for any tension or strong sensation. Once you locate the tension, see if you can soften and relax the area where you are holding stress. Notice your thoughts as your body relaxes and softens further into the earth. Meet your body and your mind with compassion. This pose is a reminder of who you are—peaceful, content, and at ease.

.... why not try

YOGA POSE

Maybe our suffering
is not what we are
carrying but how we
are carrying it.

"You've been criticizing yourself for years and it hasn't worked. Try approving of yourself and see what happens." —*Louise Hay*

Understanding the Inner Critic

Listen...do you hear it? We all have an inner critic that likes to remind us of our deepest fears. And often when we listen to that loud voice, we stay small and avoid taking risks. The critic is there to help keep us safe from pain, rejection and feeling real emotions. But what happens when we lean into physical and emotional discomfort? What happens when we face our fears head-on and try to understand them instead of just silencing them?

There's an expression, "Wherever you go, there you are." We can try to avoid sensation, but in the end, there's no protection from pain and loss. And when we understand that there's no way to avoid struggle, we can begin to build empathy for ourselves. And that's when the critic becomes quiet.
Here's an exercise to silence the critic, face your fears and start to heal...

BE BOLD

why not try......

1. **BUILD**   *awareness of the negative thoughts of the inner critic.*
2. **OPEN**   *yourself up to what the fears are.*
3. **LEAN**   *into the discomfort.*
4. **DECIDE**   *to challenge the critic by facing your fears.*
             with compassion and empathy for yourself.

If we speak to ourselves like we would to a best friend, our defenses will come down and our body will respond with ease.

It's about time to be on your own side.

Breath for Calm

Your breath is your greatest link between your mind and your body. When you steady and deepen your breath with equal length inhales and exhales, you give the body permission to soften and will the mind to focus.

However, when moving quickly through the day, you may find yourself breathing from the top of the chest. This shallow breathing with shorter inhales and exhales can be a sign of stress and can, in turn, cause stress. The sympathetic nervous system therefore kicks in and alerts the body that there is always some kind of imminent threat. Psychologist Rick Hanson calls it living "life on simmer." Living with long-term shallow breathing can put stress on all of the other systems of the body and lead to illness.

Imagine constantly speeding and breaking quickly as you drive your car. The car will certainly not run efficiently and will start to break down over time. Keeping a steady speed and maintaining a healthy engine will result in optimal performance.

The good news is that the involuntary action of breathing can be controlled. At any moment, you can slow and steady your breath to activate the parasympathetic nervous system which allows the body to find ease. So tune into your breath, slow it down and relax...you're okay, right here and right now!

Notice when you are feeling stressed.
Take a deep breath in through your nose for 4 - 3 - 2 - 1 seconds.
Exhale through your mouth for 8 - 7 - 6 - 5 - 4 - 3 - 2 - 1 seconds.
Repeat for three rounds of breath.
Notice how your body feels after just three rounds of breath.
Exhaling longer than inhaling relaxes the body.
Now, with a more relaxed body, breathe smooth and steady
with equal length inhales and equal length exhales.

...... why not try

PRANAYAMA

"If you want to conquer
the anxiety of life,
live in the moment,
live in the breath."

— *Amit Ray*

"The most common way people give up their power is by thinking they don't have any."

—*Alice Walker*

Open to Your Power

There's a Zen parable about a man walking through the woods. As he is on his merry way, he sees another man on a horse racing through the woods wildly and out of control. The man walking asks the man on the horse as he races by, "Where are you going in such a rush?" The man on the horse replies, "I don't know, ask the horse?"

In this story, the horse represents our untamed thoughts, our habits, and our subconscious leading the way and ruling our life. The man on the horse becomes a victim to himself and therefore has no purpose or direction.

Each time you tune into the present moment, you begin the powerful process of recognizing how you showed up for yourself and what is true for you. The practice of mindfulness invites you to reign in your thoughts, your words, and your actions so you can move more intentionally.

Ultimately, there are so many things that you can't control, but turn your awareness to what you can control. There is so much power in recognizing your thoughts, your words, and your actions. That connection will allow you to move purposefully, and less chaotically, through life.

why not try...... *Start by paying attention to your thoughts each day. Next, start to notice the words you choose and the tone in which you deliver them. If you are mindful of your thoughts and words, your actions will follow in a way that is intentional.*

HumanKIND

Kindness begins at home—it begins inside of you. Not only is kindness and compassion born in your actual physical home—your body—but also in your spiritual home—your highest self. There's a song called The Bones with the lyric "The house don't fall when the bones are good." When loving kindness is your foundation, and starts where you live—in your body, heart and mind—that power of compassion can expand to those who live in your house with you, to your neighbors, and beyond. So how do you access that kindness and compassion within yourself? You don't have to be perfect, you just have to pay attention.

Start by recognizing where there is a fracture in the support system. ....*why not try*
Find the struggle in the body and ask, are you fighting yourself?
Are you resisting tight areas in your body?
Are you not feeling connected?
If so, maybe try softening?
Try letting go of the war within.

Love yourself first, so you can love those around you, fully and without reservation. When you do the work to love yourself first, your connection, kindness, and compassion grows and strengthens in others.

A reminder that we are humanKIND, after all, and here for each other.

"Every act of kindness
is a piece of love
we leave behind."

—*Paul Williams*

"We can learn a lot from trees: they're always grounded but never stop reaching heavenward."

—*Everett Mamor*

Lessons From a Tree

As the seasons shift from summer to fall,
I struggle with the change.
I long for more days of the sun on my skin
and the warm gentle breezes.
As I take a walk in the woods,
I feel the brisk air,
a reminder of the inevitable cold on the way.
And then I see you, tree.

You grow in all directions.
Your roots run deep.
You're grounded and of the earth.
You know where you are from,
but you're not afraid to rise
to lengthen towards the sun,
creating new growth as your buds form
and nurture that growth from your base.

Once your leaves have fully expressed themselves,
you are not afraid to let go, without resistance.
Your leaves help to nurture the ground.
You let go, to make space
for new growth, new possibilities.

I see you.
And I realize your transition
is the very definition of grace.
Finding the beauty in letting go
without struggle.
Finding peace in the uneasy act of change.

The One You Feed

There is an old story where a grandfather tells his grandchild about two wolves who were in a battle. One is a wolf of love representing kindness, compassion, and courage. And the other is a wolf of hate representing fear, anger, and greed. As the child listened to the grandfather describe each of the wolves, she asked the elder "Which one wins?" He looked down at his grandchild and said, "The one you feed."

Both wolves exist within each of us. Our lives are determined by which wolf we feed each day. The parable suggests that we always have a choice. And that choice begins with a single thought.

In my favorite Yoga Sutra 2.33, Patanjali describes the practice of *pratipaksha-bhavana* which simply means that when negative thoughts arise, instead of following their path and diving deeper into harmful mental patterns, counter those negative thoughts with their opposite. When we choose to focus on the good, our struggles blur and recede. But we know it isn't easy to quiet that negative part of ourselves. Where there are thoughts of anger, try to cultivate thoughts of love. Where there is resentment, tune into a deeper feeling of gratitude. Where there is sadness, find the joy.

Little by little as we redirect our thoughts towards empathy and good will, we feed that wolf of love, starve the wolf of hate, and allow ourselves to let go of the separation that holds us back from real connection.

"Attitude is a choice. Happiness is a choice. Optimism is a choice. Kindness is a choice. Giving is a choice. Respect is a choice. Whatever choice you make makes you. Choose wisely."

— *Roy T. Bennett*

"Beliefs are choices. First you choose your beliefs. Then your beliefs affect your choices."

—Roy T. Bennett

Your Conscious Life

There's an expression: "Life is 10% what happens to you and 90% how you respond." We, alone, are solely responsible for our livelihood and our happiness. And we are not only responsible for our own choices, but for our own values and beliefs. So, what are values and beliefs?

Value = a person's principles or standards of behavior;
one's judgment of what is important in life

Belief = a firmly held truth, a statement one accepts as real

Every thought pattern and standard that you have is a choice. And when you choose to follow the values and beliefs of others, you unknowingly give away your power to live consciously. But when you create awareness around the existing belief systems you hold, you can choose to continue along the same path or change direction. But conscious living requires an understanding that you are 100% responsible for your thoughts, words and actions so you can make choices that support your best life.

why not try......

1. What three values are most important to you?

2. What belief that you have inherited through family or society aligns with your three most important values?

3. What is a belief that you have inherited through family or society that may be holding you back from expressing yourself fully and honestly?

4. List three beliefs based on your key values that you would like to carry into the future...

Compassion Within

We must find the compassion within ourselves for ourselves before extending that generosity out to the world.

Pema Chödrön, a Tibetan Buddhist teacher, says, "In order to have compassion for others, we have to have compassion for ourselves. In particular, to care about other people who are fearful, angry, jealous, overpowered by addictions of all kinds, arrogant, proud, miserly, selfish, mean—you name it—to have compassion and to care for these people means not to run from the pain of finding these things in ourselves."

Karuna is the Buddhist and Hindu word for compassion, reminding us that "compassionate action" starts within. Can you find compassion for yourself in your body, in your thoughts, in your words, in your practice, and in your life?

Take a deep breath in, inhaling compassion for yourself. .... *why not try?*
Take a long breath out, sending that compassion
out to the earth.
Breathe in and receive beauty, love generosity.
Breathe out and send your healing energy out to the world.
Breathe in to receive.
Breathe out to give back.

be kind

"Remember, if you ever need
a helping hand, it's at the end
of your arm. As you get older,
remember you have another hand:
The first is to help yourself,
the second is to help others."

—*Sam Levenson*

"In the beginner's mind there are many possibilities, but in the expert's there are few."

—*Shunryu Suzuki*

Beginner's Mind

A young miner who went down into the most abundant mine to look for gold.
He dug and dug and dug and all he found were dirty green metal scraps that
he kept throwing to the side. When he came out of the mine, his friends asked
him what he had found. "Agh," he said, "there was nothing there." But what he
didn't know was that those dirty green shards of metal that he discarded, were
actually oxidized gold pieces that, when treated with acid, turn into the shiny
metal that we all recognize.

When your thoughts are fixed and you only see things one way, you miss out on
the abundance that is right in front of you. When you look at the world from a
beginner's mind, the world opens up for you to receive. If you move through life
with an open mind, everything can be a miracle and so much can be gained.

why not try ....

YOGA POSE

*Child's Pose (Balasana) is a resting pose that allows you to open the hips gently and
lengthen the back. Grounding and humbling, this pose brings you back to your center
and reminds you that you can start again at any moment.*

- *Start in tabletop with your wrists under shoulders and knees under hips.*
- *Bring your toes to touch and drop your hips back to your heels.*
- *Separate your knees wide to open the hips or keep knees together to focus more
  on the rounding of the spine.*
- *Walk your hands forward and bring your forehead to the mat or onto a block.*
- *Option to keep your arms extended and hands resting on the mat,
  or send your arms back alongside the body and cup your heels with your hands.*
- *Find rest in this pose and stay as long as your needs the release.*
- *To come out of the pose, press into your hands and slowly rise to seated.*

Empathetic Listening

There are many ways to listen. The usual way we listen to each other is through 'responsive listening' where the purpose is to problem solve and create a dialogue. While one person speaks, the other forms their thoughts and responses. And usually the response is driven by the ego, which assesses, judges, and creates separation. In our yoga practice, we work towards developing that quieter empathetic listening skill. Here, we listen with a nonjudgmental mind, an open heart, and an ear for understanding. This form of deep listening encourages curiosity and creates connection and emotional intimacy.

The skill of empathetic listening begins with how we create awareness and listen to our own bodies and observe our thought patterns. When we notice the areas of tension with an open mind, we naturally soften. And from that deep internal observation, we can begin to practice deep listening with those around us. Those lucky enough to have a friend to confide in who does not judge and listens deeply know what a powerful gift it can be. So, start within and let your healing radiate to those lucky enough to be around you.

Take a moment to let go of any judgments and expectations you have and begin to quiet.

......why not try

Start with a body scan:
Notice the face, shoulders, the chest, the belly, the root...
What is your body trying to tell you?
Can you listen deeply to hear the messages?
What part of your body needs your attention?
What does this part of your body want you to understand?

Now begin to rest your awareness in your heart:
What does your heart want you to be aware of in this moment?
What does your heart want you to understand?
What does your heart want you to feel?
When you listen deeply, you give yourself and others the chance to be heard and to heal.

BODY AND HEART SCAN

"To listen is to lean in softly with the willingness to be changed by what we hear."

— *Mark Nepo*

"The two most powerful warriors are patience and time."

—*Leo Tolstoy*

Patience and Clarity

Like the rocks in the river that become smooth over time, patience is the process of letting life flow at a pace that may not follow your time schedule. When you slow down your pace, you are able to see things more clearly.

There is an old parable about when Buddha asked his student to fetch him some water from the lake down the hill. The student, of course, said yes and walked to the water only to see an oxen pulling a cart through the water making it murky and undrinkable. He returned and told the Buddha that the water was too dirty for consumption. The Buddha said nothing. A half hour later the Buddha asked the student if he would fetch him some water. The student returned to the lake but the water was still too dirty to drink. Defeated, he returned and told the Buddha that the water was still too dirty. The Buddha said nothing. A half hour later the Buddha asked the student if he would fetch him some water. By this time the student was irritated but, nevertheless, he went down to the lake as his master asked. But when he arrived the water was clear so he fetched the water and happily brought it back to the Buddha. The Buddha asked, "What did you do to make this water drinkable?" The student did not understand the question. The Buddha continued, "With patience, the mud settled on its own and the water became clear. It's the same with your thoughts. When your thoughts are disturbing your mind, find patience to still the thoughts so you can become clear and balanced."

The main way to identify patience is to recognize when you are being impatient. Sometimes I catch myself being impatient with my child. When that happens everything gets clouded and anger starts to take over my words. When I'm aware that this is happening, I pause and step away for a moment. That moment is all I needed to soothe the rough thoughts and slow the pace to meet my child where he is. Then conflict can turn to negotiation and we can both walk away calm.

Happy Self, Happy Life

Why is it that we look for love from everyone around us except ourselves? My father used to say, "If you don't expect anything from others, you won't be disappointed." I always found that statement to be a little depressing. But because he never had high expectations from others, when anyone would do something kind or generous for him, he would be extremely grateful.

As you get older, the idea of self-care becomes increasingly important. When you are not reliant on others for your own happiness, then anything another does for you is just icing on your already sweet cake.

A few years ago, Mother's Day was approaching and it didn't seem like that my preteen boys would make me feel warm and fuzzy. So, I decided to take Mother's Day into my own hands and take a weekend getaway out West with a friend and fellow mother. I ended up in Scottsdale, Arizona. I climbed a mountain by myself and spent the rest of the weekend with my girlfriend enjoying the sunshine, swimming in the pool, and eating delicious food. When I returned home, I was so very thankful to receive beautiful white tulips and a card that my boys made for me while I was away. If I hadn't taken the steps to nurture and feed myself, I might have been left expecting and wanting more. But because my heart was full by the time I got home anything I received from my family was the icing on my already sweet cake.

Here's what I learned about choosing my own self-care: ....*note to self*

1. *Don't be afraid to be alone.*
2. *Do things that make you happy.*
3. *Learn how to say no.*
4. *Care less about what others think.*
5. *Only you know what you need.*

"Peace begins
when expectation ends."

—Sri Chinmoy

"It is in the smallest details, and the simplest words that we can connect to the greatest truths."

—Chris Trapper

The Craft of Songwriting

My husband is a singer/songwriter so I have witnessed, for many
years, the craft of songwriting. Occasionally I have assisted with the
placement of a lyric or two. There is an expression in the industry that
songwriters despise: "Don't bore us, get to the chorus." The idea is
that the average listener just wants to get to the catchiest
part of the song.

But just like in life, the real artistry and wisdom comes from the verses
leading up to the chorus, or the main event. The perfect word choice
that creates room for interpretation within the buildup can be
where the magic of the song is realized and felt the most. The chorus
might be powerful and memorable just like the major moments in your
life... graduation, marriage, having children, vacations.
But what about the rest of it?

We have two events that will certainly happen to all of us, birth and
death. And the rest? It's all transition. Don't let it pass unappreciated
and unlived...

note to self...... *Let's not wait for the chorus to sing. Sing now.*
Let's not wait for the wedding to dance. Dance right here.
Let's not wait for the yoga class to breathe. Inhale and exhale longer.

You Are the Sun

You are the sun.
You are powerful beyond measure.
You are life-giving.
You nurture those around you.
You bring warmth and love to the world.
You lift everyone's mood.
You are pure energy.
You radiate and shine.

But then the clouds come.
And they feel more powerful than you.
They dim your spirit and hold you back.
They cause you to question your authentic self.
They bring you into darkness.
And make the ground feel heavier.
The weight is sometimes too much to bear.

But you are the sun.
You are life-giving.
And you are forever.
And when you harness that power,
the clouds have nothing to say
and away they float to bring their struggle to another star.
They are temporary and you are forever.

You are the sun.

"Keep your face to the
sun and you will never
see the shadows."
—Helen Keller

"When you allow this moment to be enough, it doesn't mean you stop working on what you want your life to be, it just means you are opening your heart to a more joyful life right now." —*Allison Carmen*

You are enough

Wandering Mind

It's not always easy to be truly present... for our families, loved ones and especially for ourselves. Harvard University psychologists Matthew Killingsworth and Daniel T. Gilbert created an app that asked 2,250 volunteers to track their happiness. Their subsequent paper "A Wandering Mind Is an Unhappy Mind," concluded that people were less happy when they were not present and focused on the activity at hand—they were not happy when their minds were wandering. And the data showed that our minds wander around 46.9% of the time—that's almost half of our lives. I find that my tendency is not to live in the past, but to spend much of my time in the future. My husband jokes with me that I don't have a good memory because I'm always thinking about what's next. How can I better myself? What more can I be doing? What next? And, conversely, we all know someone who's holding onto the past tightly and won't let go.

But the mindfulness practice is a reminder to wake up to what is right in front of us, to slow down enough to catch up. There is a *Bodhisattva* (Buddhist saint) aspiration/prayer: "May whatever circumstances arise serve the awakening of all hearts." Paying attention to the now is a way to awaken the heart and find acceptance to wherever you are in this moment.

why not try......

HAND MUDRA

Jnana Mudra
The Sanskrit word Jnana translates to "wisdom" and the word mudra. means "hand gesture." This mudra helps to create focus, acceptance and connection by bringing the thumb, which represents universal consciousness, and the index finger, which represents individual consciousness, together. Here's what to do:

1. Sit comfortably, resting the backs of your palms onto your knees.

2. Bring your index fingers to under the tips of your thumbs and allow the other three fingers to gently extend out.

3. Close your eyes and feel the deep connection with yourself and the greater world around you.

Stay Awake

Are you awake? Or are you constantly just coasting through your day? I often catch myself in the middle of the day asking where the morning went. Was I just on autopilot, driving around, getting things done without being mindful in the least? Time can move so quickly and if we don't stop to smell the roses or even the hot coffee cup in our hand, we can miss out on everything.

The practice asks us to wake up to where we are, right here, right now in this present moment. Why? Because when you are truly present everything is clear and available to you. The smallest thing reveals itself to be a miracle. Find a blade of grass and really examine it with your fingers. Or maybe taste a single summer blueberry in all of the regions of your mouth. When you keep a beginner's heart, you can't help but be truly awake. And when you practice with that open mindfulness, you meet yourself where you are, find compassion for yourself, and then maybe discover yourself all over again. It all begins now... so stay awake!

why not try...... | *Think of a chore that is mundane and uninteresting to you. The next time you perform the chore, see if you can activate all of your senses and bring awareness to the actual task at hand.*

Here's an example: If you are doing the dishes, take time to notice how the water feels on your hands. Notice the temperature of the water, the speed with which the water is pouring out of the spout, the sound that the water makes as it hits the inside of the sink. Feel the texture of the sponge and take a moment to smell the soap as you pour it onto the sponge, allowing the sponge to soften and absorb the soap. Take time to explore your senses and appreciate the smallest of tasks.

"Those who are
awake live in a
state of constant
amazement."

— *Jack Kornfield*

"Happiness cannot
be traveled to, owned,
earned, worn or consumed.
Happiness is the spiritual
experience of living every
minute with love, grace
and gratitude."

—*Denis Waitley*

Happiness Now

You are responsible for your own happiness. Happiness is not something that comes later in life. If you are waiting to lose 10 pounds, or receive a paycheck, or go on vacation in order to discover happiness, you may never find it.

In the yoga practice, "sukha" means ordinary happiness. I used to find so much joy in the early spring when I would walk in the woods and discover a pink lady slipper along the path. But that joy instantly turned into "duhkha" or suffering when the next time I took my walk the lady slipper was gone. When you rely on external conditions for your happiness outside of yourself, you will never maintain equanimity. The practice of yoga takes you to a deeper level of understanding true happiness that comes from inside yourself. "Santosha" means contentment or ease. It's a choice to be conscious, and to be ok wherever you are. Santosha teaches you that there's nothing you need beyond yourself to make you happy.

Awareness of the present moment will allow you to open up to all of the joys and contentment that you could ever want. And the good news is, that happiness is available at any moment. So tune in and allow yourself to receive. Your joy is already here...

why not try......

Whatever you are doing STOP and take a moment to:

1. Look around in all directions. What do you see?

2. Take a deep breath through your nose. What do you smell?

3. For the next 10 seconds listen intently. What do you hear?

4. Can you feel the clothes that you are wearing on your skin?

5. What is the taste in your mouth?

Now smile as wide as you can.
This is YOU truly present for this moment.

Food is Love

When I reflect upon my fondest loving memories of my past, more than half of them are centered around meals with loved ones. Generosity of the spirit has always been the most important value within my personal system of beliefs. And what better way to show generosity than by making and sharing delicious and healthy food that honors tradition and makes those around you feel loved. Hummos and Arabic chips have always been a staple in my Palestinian-American home. By sharing the recipe, my hope is to share a little piece of my heart. Enjoy!

Hania's Hummos Recipe

2 cans of chick peas (reserve 1-2 tbsp for garnish)

3 tbsp tahini sauce

3 cloves of garlic

1 tsp salt

3 tbsp fresh lemon juice

Paprika (for garnish)

Extra virgin olive oil

In a food processor. blend the first five ingredients together.
Add olive oil or water to achieve desired consistency.
Spread in a shallow bowl.
Garnish with reserved chick peas, paprika and olive oil.

Serve with Arabic bread cut into bite-sized pieces, drizzled with
olive oil, salt, pepper, and nutritional yeast and
baked at 375° until golden brown.

......why not try

RECIPE

"The people who give you their food give you their heart."
—Cesar Chavez

"There is no better
antidote to perfectionism
than the knowledge that
you already have what
you're looking for."

—*Sally Kempton*

The Art of Imperfection

The Japanese word "Wabi-sabi" represents the idea of imperfection as the truest beauty. The idea is based on the Buddhist teachings that everything is transient in nature and therefore incomplete or imperfect. Japanese aesthetics are based on this principle. And artisans will even intentionally add a flaw to an otherwise perfect piece to illustrate that philosophy.

In the West, we strive for perfection in so many ways—and often we are left feeling inadequate. Perfectionism is just the desire to feel whole and complete. Our yoga practice reminds us that we are already there. With all our flaws, with all our self-doubt, we are perfect. *Santosha*, which means contentment, is one of the *Niyamas* in the *Yoga Sutras by Patanjali*. It illustrates that blissful place of finding acceptance and contentment with exactly where you are.

"By contentment, the highest happiness is attained."
— The Yoga Sutras of Patanjali, Sutra II.42

So... why not let go of self-imposed unrealistic expectations and truly start living with acceptance and ease?

Weight of the World

As you sit still, you may notice that you have been carrying more weight and heaviness in your body and mind than what's necessary to keep you grounded. Sometimes it is that weight that blocks you from living with ease in your life. However, you may be able to release that heaviness simply by cultivating awareness of where the tightness exists in your body. One of my favorite moments when I'm teaching a yoga class is in the beginning when I observe all of the students as they sit in sacred space with their eyes closed. When I instruct them to notice their breath, at least half of the class deepen their breath. It just happens. Energy follows intention. And the more we live with intention and awareness, the more we can let go of the weight we are holding onto and the more we can move into ease.

*Here's a **chakra meditation** to release the weight of the world and find ease.*

Find a comfortable seat, rooting through your sitting bones and with your spine long. Close your eyes or soften your gaze on one spot. Notice and follow your natural breath. Next, bring all of your awareness to your body. Start by focusing your energy on your root, your sitting bones. Let yourself feel grounded and supported in this moment where you are. Breathe here and visualize a warm red glow—you are safe and secure. Start to draw your energy upward to right below your navel. Tune in to your emotions in this moment. Give yourself permission to let go of any emotions that are weighing you down. Visualize a warm orange glow. Now imagine the orange turning to yellow as you keep drawing your awareness up above the navel to your solar plexus. Breathe into your belly as you tap into the power of your gut. Bring that strength with you as you move upwards towards your heart. Visualize a green glow softening the space around your heart and finding compassion for yourself. Let your energy rise, picturing the color blue and breathe deeply to clear your throat so you can live your life speaking your truth. Continue your journey up to the third eye, your forehead, and take some time here to build your concentration and open your mind to your inner wisdom. Picture a calm cool indigo light. And let that light transition into a violet hue and eventually to white. You are open to all of the happiness that is within you. You are light itself. When you are ready to release the meditation, simply open your eyes.

...... why not try

CHAKRA
MEDITATION

- .... CROWN CHAKRA
- .... THIRD EYE CHAKRA
- .... THROAT CHAKRA
- .... HEART CHAKRA
- .... SOLAR PLEXUS CHAKRA
- .... SACRAL CHAKRA
- .... ROOT CHAKRA

Our bodies and our minds are designed to bear weight, but that doesn't mean we need to keep holding in everything we accumulate along the way.

"It's a transformative experience to simply pause instead of immediately filling up space."

— *Pema Chodron*

Fear of Space

Sometimes it feels safer to stay busy than to face whatever is lying underneath the surface. It's easy to get lost in the world of work and daily obligations. Time and space then seem like enemies that we are trying to outwit or outpace.

When I was in art school, my painting teacher used to repeat the Latin phrase 'horror vacui', which translates to 'fear of empty space.' She would critique young painters as they tried to fill up every part of the canvas with detail and imagery, explaining that the negative space—the absence of image—was just as important as what was there. The negative space allowed the painting to breathe. It's the same concept in music. The rest is just as important as the notes. Without the rest, the music would just be noise. It is the spaces of silence that give the sounds their weight and meaning.

It takes courage and discipline to pause and create space from the busyness of life. But it is in that pause where we can take a breath, check in and face the music, so to speak. The pause builds our power and our ability to respond, not from fear, but from wisdom.

why not try

YOGA POSE

*One yoga pose which I believe accesses our courage is **bridge pose** (Setu Bandha Sarvangasana). Here's how to move into this pose:*
1. *Lie on your back, bend your knees and plant your feet hip-width under your knees.*
2. *Bring your hands alongside your body with your palms firmly planted on the ground.*
3. *Root down into your hands and feet, engage your back body (squeeze your glutes) and lift your hips high.*
4. *Keep the hips lifted and breathe. It takes courage to breathe into your heart, so fire up the breath so you can hear it for a few rounds.*
5. *Slowly release your hips down to the floor and take a few breaths here.*

Cozy Time

The Danish word *hygge* (pronounced Hue-Guh) is a feeling about a moment in time to appreciate a simple everyday act. The Danes are known to live well and find everyday joy by savoring the small things. My simple hygge happens upon waking up and making myself a hot drink (usually a latte), finding a cozy spot in the house to sit and appreciate each sip without distraction. This reminder to appreciate the small things with presence, gratitude and without haste is what hygge is all about. The uplifting practice brings happiness and ease to each day. Is there something you do each day that you can turn into a hygge practice?

There's a healthy, cozy **Ayurvedic tonic** *I often make to reduce inflammation, improve digestion, and detoxify the system. I usually make a batch and store it in an airtight pitcher in the fridge. Consume it cold, or heat it in a mug and enjoy it warm and cozy. Here's the recipe:*

......*why not try*

RECIPE

In a large pot on the stove combine the following ingredients:

2-3   *cinnamon sticks*

1 tsp cloves

1 tsp black peppercorns

1 tbsp   green cardamon

3-4   *slices tumeric root*

1/4 c   sliced ginger root

In a deep pasta pot on the stove, combine all the above ingredients with 1 gallon of water.
Boil water and ingredients for 10 minutes, and then let it steep in the pot for an hour.
Let it cool and strain into pitcher and store in the fridge.
Add honey if you want sweetness.

"We cannot all do great things. But we can do small things with great love."

— *Mother Teresa*

79

You can't take a breath in the past and you can't take a breath in the future. So let your breath ground you and bring you peace right now.

Little Simple Things

When things feel too big, go small.
Think of a little thing that feeds you,
that lights you up.
Just a little thing.
Enjoying your favorite piece of music
with your eyes closed.
Taking five minutes out of your day
for nothing but quiet.
Walking across the parking lot to your car,
with a little extra joy in your step.
Noticing bright green moss
growing on a tree on a hike in the woods.
Savoring every bite of a meal,
even if it's just a simple sandwich.

When everything seems overwhelming,
It's the little things that remind us
that we are okay right here and right now.
And we can get through anything,
one beautiful breath at a time.

No Mud, No Lotus

The first Noble Truth in Buddhism is that suffering (*dukkha* in Sanskrit) exists. A beautiful illustration of our understanding of suffering comes from the symbology around the lotus flower in Buddhist and Hindu art. The lotus flower is rooted in the mud of the murkiest of ponds. As it grows it moves through the mud and the muck to eventually blossom at the water's surface. The lotus teaches us that the mud and struggles that we encounter along the way serve to teach us and add to our own awakening. It is through our struggles that we know happiness, cultivate empathy and find our resilience.

Just like the lotus flower, we didn't come into this world in an easy and pretty way. We were born from tension and covered in our own kind of mud. Our first voice was a cry. We knew as soon as we began that life would not be easy. But life is courage. It is resilience in action. When we find a way to accept and learn from our own suffering, we become more powerful. And with that power comes a deeper understanding of ourselves and others. We become more empathetic and compassionate. We understand that everyone struggles and our own struggle is the key to recognizing the vulnerability within each of us. The mud connects us to each other, enabling us to experience our shared humanity.

There is a Tibetan mantra to honor the lotus flower and the struggle within each of us. **Om mani padme hum**, loosely translates to "the jewel is in the lotus." Here's how to recite the mantra:

1. Sit comfortably on a cushion cross-legged or on a chair with your feet planted on the ground.
2. Take a few moments to regulate your breathing and find stillness.
3. Recite the mantra "om mani padme hum" to yourself or out loud as many times as you wish. And as you recite the mantra imagine sending compassion and love to all beings.
4. When you are done reciting the mantra, take a few moments to return back to your breath.

......why not try

MANTRA

"Most people are afraid of suffering. But suffering is a kind of mud to help the lotus flower of happiness grow. There can be no lotus flower without the mud."

—*Thich Nhat Hanh*

"When any real progress is made, we unlearn and learn anew what we thought we knew before."

— *Henry David Thoreau*

Unlearning

When we take a step back or look outside of ourselves, we can see more clearly. And maybe at that point, we can examine our usual ways of thinking and conditioning. That's when we see what type of behaviors we inherited from our parents and from our society. The yoga practice wakes us up, like a brand new sunrise, to all that is good in our lives, but also sheds light on what has not been working well for us and holding us back. These are the patterns that, through awareness and effort, we can change and even "un-learn."

Past behaviors ......

In the process of un-learning, ask yourself the following questions:
— *What are three patterns or ideas that I am aware of within myself?*
— *Where do these patterns or ideas come from?*
— *Are they true to my essence and my highest self?*
— *Are there any patterns or behaviors that I have been living with that no longer support my goals and principles?*

Once you trace your patterns and ways of thinking, you can then steer the ship in a different direction and un-learn repetitive unhealthy habits that prevent you from being your truest, most joyful self. So think about how your life today could be even more supported if you were to create your own values or ethics and decide to live by them.

Future behaviors ......

To promote a healthy future, ask yourself the following questions:
— *What patterns or ideas would I choose for myself today?*
— *How do they reflect who I am and who I aspire to be?*
— *Do they align with and support my overall well-being (in my life now and in the future)?*

Light Your Light

Sometimes we are afraid of our own light. Of being exposed. But it's our light that heals others. I find that the more vulnerable I become in a relationship, the closer I feel to that friend. When we're unafraid to be real, to move beyond the surface, and to let our guard down, that is when real connection can begin.

In her book *Journey to the Heart*, Melody Beattie writes:
"Step out into the cool night air. Look at the stars. See how they shine. Know that it is okay for you to shine too. Who told you you had to hold back? Who told you your gifts, your talents, your beauty—your natural, beautiful, loving, delightful self—was wrong? Who told you not to be all you could be? Maybe, as some suggest, we've gotten too comfortable focusing on our flaws, our errors, our dark side. Perhaps it's not our dark side we fear. Perhaps we are really afraid of our gifts, our brilliance, our light."

Now is a time of light. A time to shine without fear or trepidation. When you allow yourself to be truly seen, you can find intimacy with yourself and your dearest loved ones. When you tune into your light, your true nature, your heart radiates and welcomes whoever is in your path. Let your light shine for all the world to see.

Close your eyes...   .... *why not try*
Look for the heaviness. Can you feel it in your body?
Look for the heavy thoughts that you carry with you.
Don't judge them or yourself.
Observe your heaviness and light with compassion.
Welcome your vunerability with an open heart.
Now open your eyes and gaze up at the sky.
Sometimes the simple act of looking up
will shift and elevate your perspective.

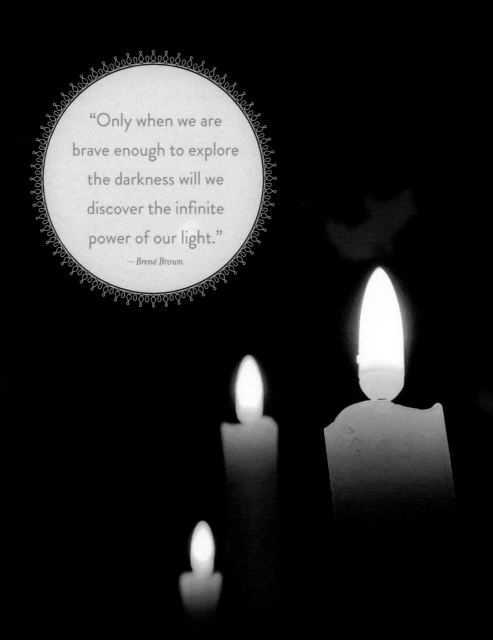

"Only when we are brave enough to explore the darkness will we discover the infinite power of our light."

— *Brené Brown*

"You owe it to everyone
you love to find pockets
of tranquility in your
busy world."

— *George Bernanos*

Tranquility in Uncertainty

During this busy time, remember who you are. Remember that the more you allow the challenges of the time to inhabit space in your heart, the less space you have to be productive and centered. Stress is the mental argument that you have with yourself. It robs you of peace and eventually turns to worry.

Finding tranquility in the chaos is the task during these transitional times when things are uncertain and routines are not yet formed. But it takes just a single moment to return to your natural state of compassionate awareness.

why not try......

MANTRA

When you feel overwhelmed, invite a mantra into your consciousness to feel grounded. A mantra is "an instrument of the mind." It is a simple and powerful phrase that, when repeated, brings focus and ease.

Here's one that I use when the world feels like it's moving too fast around me and I'm having a hard time keeping up:

I AM CENTERED AND SUPPORTED IN MY BEING

1. *Find a comfortable seat and close your eyes.*
2. *Bring your hands onto your knees or thighs and let them face down.*
3. *Repeat the mantra three times.*
4. *Listen to three or four rounds of breath.*

Notice how you feel afterwards—and whether this simple exercise changed your perspective from stress to calm.

Wild River

The autumn arrives in a fury.
The warmth of the summer sun,
more distant now.
The pace begins,
as the demands grow.
We work in busyness.
We sleep with restlessness.
There is too much to do,
in this race that we didn't want to run.

Even though the days are long,
there isn't any time.
Pushing against the winds,
we keep it together and soldier on,
hoping for a break in the clouds.

But eventually we must stop.
Eventually we find stillness,
in between all the rapid movement.
And that is when it becomes quite clear,
that a moment can ease the struggle.
A breath can create a field of space.
A thought can slow down this wild river.

Here is where we return to who we are.
We decide to meet the pace
of our lives with steadiness.
It's in the space of a single moment,
that we remember to live with ease.

Maybe then our expectations can soften.
Maybe then our compassion
for ourselves can grow.
Maybe in a single moment,
a pause, amidst a whirling life.

"Between stimulus and response
there is a space. In that space
is our power to choose our response.
In our response lies our growth
and our freedom."

—*Viktor E. Frankl*

"Rituals keep us from
forgetting what must not
be forgotten and keep us rooted
in a past from which we must
not be disconnected."

— *Tony Campolo*

Everyday Ritual

A few years back, I was fortunate to travel to India to visit with multiple Hindu families and observe how each family worships. They each maintain an area in their home with a display of the family's favorite deity, along with images and sculptures of other Hindu gods. Even if their home is small, they carve out space. Offerings of fruit and flowers are made each morning and removed each night. There are many rituals around even entering into the prayer room. Worshippers clean themselves and ceremonial dress is worn by many to show respect for the Gods. The ceremonial daily ritual of honoring gods with offerings is called "puja," the word derivative of the word "pu" which loosely translates to flower. Rich and poor alike incorporate gratitude and offering into each day.

The wisdom traditions are steeped in ritual, but how in modern society can we feel connected to something greater and find a deeper sense of belonging? When I returned home, I started to examine the daily rituals in my own life. And although I'm not driven by a particular deity or god, the work of rituals allows one to feel grounded. Rituals humble us and bring us comfort as well as increase our feelings of gratitude about life. Think about milestone rituals that we perform in our Western culture—birthday celebrations, graduations, weddings, funerals, holidays, family vacations. And now think about everyday rituals like making a cup of coffee in the morning, meditating, going to the gym, cooking dinner, etc. A ritual doesn't have to be a special occasion, it can be a simple act that incorporates the following components:

why not try......

In order for a ritual to be fully effective it must be...

1.   *Intellectually satisfying*
2.   *Emotionally fulfilling*
3.   *Have a marked moment at the beginning*
4.   *Have a strong ending*

Can you list the rituals in your life? Or can you create a new daily ritual that will allow you to feel centered and connected?

Four Locks, Four Keys

The lyrics from the song "The Gambler," which was written by Don Schlitz but famously recorded and performed by Kenny Rogers, considers the psyche of a gambler strategizing his next move by reading the room.

> "You've got to know when to hold 'em / Know when to fold 'em
> Know when to walk away / And know when to run"

It's a valuable skill to study people and situations and to be able to respond skillfully. And it's not always easy to know when to engage, when to walk away, and when to run. One of my favorite yoga teachers, Jacqui Bonwell, used to say in class, *"You don't have to say yes to every fight that you are invited to."* So when do we show compassion and when do we protect our heart? How do we deal with jealousy? Yoga Sutra 1.33 provides a practical guideline for relating to others in the world, defined by four locks and the four keys. Sri Swami Satchidananda interpreted these lessons to be:

> "By cultivating attitudes of
> friendliness toward the happy,
> compassion for the unhappy,
> delight in the virtuous,
> and disregard toward the wicked,
> the mind stuff retains its undisturbed calmness."

So let's take the first and most straightforward one "friendliness toward the happy." Obviously if someone is joyful, it's easy for you to be happy with them. The second one is also easy because when someone is suffering or unfortunate, you will want to show compassion and love. The third one is more difficult. It is all about jealousy. Can you delight in another's success without letting it be a reflection upon yourself and causing your own suffering? In other words can you separate your ego enough to truly be happy for that person? That is the challenge. The last one of the four locks, also challenging, gives you the key (permission) to disengage from the toxic people in your life. Maybe that's when you walk away or even run from those who keep draining you of your kind energy with their harmful words and actions. When we use these keys, we can move with equanimity through the world.

"A very little key
will open a very
heavy door."

— *Charles Dickens*

"Keep your face to the sunshine and you cannot see the shadows. It's what the sunflowers do."

— *George Bernanos*

Giving and Receiving

We learn from the young sunflower whose stem shifts and elongates so it can face the warmth of the sun throughout the day. One side of the plant stem extends and lengthens during the day, its face tracking the path of the sun from east to west. And at night the other side of the stem elongates to position the sunflower back in place facing east for the sunrise to begin its track again. It's a beautiful and generous practice of giving and receiving. And though one side gives so the other can receive, the whole plant benefits and becomes stronger, preparing itself to mature to a fixed position facing the east. The sunflower intuitively knows that turning towards the light will bring nourishment, healing and growth to the entire plant.

What can we learn from the sunflower plant?
1. *When you give of yourself to others, you will also benefit.*
2. *When you follow the path of warmth and light,*
   it will lead you towards strength and growth.

why not try......

YOGA POSE

Think about the ways you give to others in your life. Take a few moments to write down all the wonderful ways others receive your generosity and attention.

Now let's experience giving and receiving within our own bodies:

Cow / Cat Tilt
· *Start in tabletop with your wrists under shoulders and knees under hips.*
· *Spread your fingers wide and press into your hands.*
· *Inhale, let your belly drop and look up, expanding through the chest.*
· *Exhale, press into your hands and round the spine, drop your head.*
· *Repeat for a few rounds, linking your breath to your movement.*

STEP 1   STEP 2

Focus on the Good

Our inherent nature is peaceful and content. But our life and the struggles we own and create can separate us from our very center. Sometimes our struggles are there to wake us up to what we need to do and push us to take action in our lives. But if we focus too sharply on those struggles, our hearts and minds feel that weight and become heavy. We become driven by that loud egoic voice within that always judges, critiques and casts a shadow on our current state. And although the ego could have positive aspects and fuel personal and professional growth, when we are only responding to that voice, we create separation from our present joy. We move from a place of scarcity rather than abundance, and from negativity rather than inner peace.

In the affluent suburb where I live, my home is considered relatively modest. In the context of the whole world, I am extremely comfortable and secure. But everything is relative. When comparing myself to my neighbors with multiple homes and overflowing bank accounts, I could easily feel the tug of envy and discontent. But instead, I choose to wake up grateful for the beauty and love that I have around me. In the first scene from the film "The Shift" by Wayne Dyer, he wakes up, sits on his bed and says to the universe "Thank you. Thank you. Thank you." What a way to start the day, with an abundance of gratitude!

When you focus on what you have rather than what you lack, you not only diffuse the ego, but build-up that reserve of happiness. It is that attitude of gratitude that brings more joy into your day and to the relationships around you. The biggest gift you can give yourself is the ability to appreciate more, so ultimately you suffer less.

"The happiest people don't have the best of everything, they make the best of everything."

— *Oprah Winfrey*

99

"The reason we struggle
with insecurity is because
we compare our behind
the scenes with everyone
else's highlight reel."

— *Steve Furtick*

Your Path to Walk

There have been a few "aha" moments in my life where something small happened to shift my perspective and lead me to a different path. One such moment was when I was in middle school, in the height of my insecurities at 13 years old, trying to discover who I was and how to fit in. Growing up ethnic in a very preppy town in the 1980s had its challenges. I remember my deep desire for belonging paired with an equal need for self-expression. One day, I found myself in the preppiest clothing store and decided that I would try to fit in once and for all. So I grabbed a button down shirt, some beige khakis, and a printed whale belt and went into the dressing room to put it all together. The "aha" moment came when I walked out of the stall to look at the mirror. I begin laughing hysterically at the outfit that was completely ridiculous on me. Then I decided that this was not going to be the way to fit in.

In that moment, I realized that maybe I was not the preppiest or the prettiest by someone else's standards, but I have my own style. So I began to dress for my body and express myself fully with more alternative clothing. And as I started feeling more comfortable I noticed people started buying the same pieces of clothing that I was showcasing around school. And somewhere between the whale belt and the Doc Martins, I found my confidence. From that moment on, I decided to forge my own path and not be afraid to laugh at myself along the way.

why not try......

— *Acknowledge the insecurities within.*
— *Explore where the feelings are coming from:*
  · *Am I insecure about my own financial state?*
  · *Do I not see my own unique beauty?*
  · *Is my relationship not strong and secure enough?*
  · *How confident am I with the path that I am on?*
— *Study if the feelings of inadequacy seem true or exaggerated.*
— *Separate yourself from the feeling and find gratitude for what you have and who you are.*

Looking Back with Compassion

I almost forgot to take my son to his chorus concert one night—something I would have regretted. But we made it. There was no trophy, no high five, no special acknowledgement for getting him there. Just another unrecognized moment in raising children, with the usual feeling of being behind the eight-ball.

Back when I was in the throes of young motherhood, an older yoga student of mine who could sense my exhaustion shared the old adage, "The days are long, but the years are short." Over the years I've had my fair share of wallowing in the "What did I miss?" and "Am I doing enough?" There's a beautiful, messy vulnerability to caregiving; often challenging to the core, yet powerfully expanding the heart in all directions. And with each long day, the more deeply I loved, the more vulnerable I became. With that openness came an undiscovered resilience, carrying me through the difficult days and holding me gently during the long nights.

Buddhists say that birds need two wings to fly, one wing represents wisdom and the other compassion. Wisdom is the deep understanding of the reality of the moment and compassion is being able to empathize and meet the moment with lovingkindness. Just as both wings are needed to fly in a straight line, both wings are needed to raise a child. When vulnerability and insight meet with love and compassion, a resilience forms and takes flight.

So at some point, you just have to decide to put the calendar and the criticism down and remind yourself that you are doing the best you can. And maybe years from now in "kindsight" you will realize that you did a pretty darn good job.

"Kindsight is viewing
life experiences with
tenderness and
understanding."
— *Tara Cousineau*

"When life is not coming
up roses, look to the weeds
and find the beauty hidden
within them."

—L. F. Young

In the Weeds

How many hours have you spent picking weeds from a stone patio or cutting your grass short to remove them? On their best day, weeds are considered a nuisance. But why? And how do we as humans draw such a definitive line in the soil between desired plant and troublesome invader? Well, weeds by definition are wild plants that grow in a cultivated area, causing crops to struggle and choke. They irritate humans and even induce illness. No wonder they're considered pests. But if we examine our history, we might credit weeds for our survival as a species. Before the domestication of plants 10,000 years ago, weeds were the primary source of plant food. Our hunter and gatherer ancestors depended on the wild plants for existence. Once we learned to cultivate, harvest, and control our own environment, our disdain for weeds commenced.

In his book, *Weeds: In Defense of Nature's Most Unloved Plants*, Richard Mabey wrote, "[Weeds] are unfussy about where they live, adapt quickly to environmental stress, use multiple strategies for getting their own way. It's curious that it took so long for us to realize that the species they most resemble is us."

Maybe weeds strike a chord within us because we see ourselves in their relentless quest for survival. If we let go of our need for order and selection and look to our common traits, we might gain insight into our own resilience. In studying weeds, we might learn more about our own strengths and perseverance. And then maybe, just maybe, we might see their unique and distinctive beauty.

Rest & Return

The world is spinning. *Yes.*
So much sadness & anger out there. *Yes.*
There's not enough time. *Yes.*
You're not where you want to be. *Yes.*
You might even feel depleted. *Yes.*
Don't quit.
Rest.

Take on too much? *Yes.*
Get down on yourself for those last 10 pounds? *Yes.*
Sometimes think you're a terrible parent? *Yes.*
Compromise your health for your schedule? *Yes.*
Never feel like enough? *Yes.*
Don't quit.
Rest.

It's in the rest where you see your struggles.
It's in the moment of reckoning where a change can be a choice.
A choice to return to the values that mirror your highest self.
The return to you — when you make the powerful choice
not to quit,
but to rest.

"There is renewal
in rest."

—*Lailah Gifty Akita*

SUN SALUTATION A VARIATION *(Surya Namaskar)*

IN = Inhale / EX = Exhale

	From Down Dog *(Adho Mukha Svanasana)*
IN	Bend Knees / Look Forward
EX	Step or Hop to Front of Mat
IN	Half Lift *(Ardha Uttanasana)*
EX	Fold Forward *(Uttanasana)*
IN	Rise to Standing, Arms High Baby Backbend
EX	Hands to Heart
IN	Rise to Standing
EX	Fold Forward *(Uttanasana)*
IN	Half Lift *(Ardha Uttanasana)*
EX	High to Low Pushup *(Chatturanga Dandasana)*
IN	Upward Facing Dog *(Urdhva Mukha Svanasana)*
EX	Downward Facing Dog *(Adho Mukha Svanasana)*

SUN SALUTATION B VARIATION *(Surya Namaskar)*

IN = Inhale / EX = Exhale

	From Mountain Pose *(Tadasana)*
IN	Bend Knees. Sink Hips, Arms High — Chair Pose *(Utkatasana)*
EX	Fold Forward *(Uttanasana)*
IN	Half Lift *(Ardha Uttanasana)*
EX	High to Low Pushup *(Chatturanga Dandasana)*
IN	Upward Facing Dog *(Urdhva Mukha Svanasana)*
EX	Downward Facing Dog *(Adho Mukha Svanasana)*
IN	Step Right Forward, Rise to Warrior 1 *(Virabhadrasana A)*
EX	High to Low Pushup *(Chatturanga Dandasana)*
IN	Upward Facing Dog *(Urdhva Mukha Svanasana)*
EX	Downward Facing Dog *(Adho Mukha Svanasana)*
IN	Step Left Forward, Rise to Warrior 1 *(Virabhadrasana A)*
EX	High to Low Pushup *(Chatturanga Dandasana)*
IN	Upward Facing Dog *(Urdhva Mukha Svanasana)*
EX	Downward Facing Dog *(Adho Mukha Svanasana)*
IN	Half Lift *(Ardha Uttanasana)*
EX	Fold Forward *(Uttanasana)*
IN	Bend Knees. Sink Hips, Arms High — Chair Pose *(Utkatasana)*
EX	Mountain Pose *(Tadasana)*

Choose a leader for the group who can create a safe and open environment. Everyone take five minutes to read and answer question #1. The leader then calls on each willing participant to share their thoughts as the group listens empathetically. When everyone has been heard, the leader asks everyone to move on to the next question and sets the timer for five minutes and repeats the sharing circle for each question.

WEEK TWENTY-THREE — YOUR CONSCIOUS LIFE

1. What three values are most important to you?

2. What belief that you have inherited through family or society aligns with your three most important values?

3. What is a belief that you have inherited through family or society that is holding you back from expressing yourself fully?

4. List three beliefs based on your key values that you would like to carry into the future...

One last thing... don't forget to live the life you love. ♥